# P·I·C·T·U·R·E·P·E·D·I·A

## NOTE TO PARENTS

This book is part of PICTUREPEDIA, a completely
new kind of information series for children.
Its unique combination of pictures and words
encourages children to use their eyes to discover and
explore the world, while introducing them to a wealth
of basic knowledge. Clear, straightforward text
explains each picture thoroughly and provides
additional information about the topic.

"Looking it up" becomes an easy task with
PICTUREPEDIA, an ideal first reference for all types of
schoolwork. Because PICTUREPEDIA is also entertaining,
children will enjoy reading its words and looking
at its pictures over and over again. You can encourage
and stimulate further inquiry by helping your child
pose simple questions for the whole family to
"look up" and answer together.

# MAMMALS

**DK**

A DK PUBLISHING BOOK

**Consultant** Martyn Bramwell
**Project Editor** Sarah Miller
**Art Editor** Flora Awolaja
**U.S. Editor** B. Alison Weir
**Series Editor** Sarah Phillips
**Series Art Editor** Paul Wilkinson
**Picture Researcher** Miriam Sharland
**Production Manager** Ian Paton
**Production Assistant** Harriet Maxwell
**Editorial Director** Jonathan Reed
**Design Director** Ed Day

First American edition, 1993
4 6 8 10 9 7 5 3

Published in the United States by
DK Publishing, Inc., 95 Madison Avenue
New York, New York 10016

**Library of Congress Cataloging-in-Publication Data**
Bramwell, Martyn.
  Mammals / by Martyn Bramwell. — 1st American ed.
    p.   cm. — (Picturepedia)
  Includes index.
  Summary: Text and illustrations present information about the
physical characteristics and habits of all kinds of mammals.
  ISBN 1-56458-386-4
  1. Mammals—Miscellanea—Juvenile literature.   [1. Mammals.]
I. Title:  II. Series.
QL706.2.B72  1993
599—dc20                                                    93-4336
                                                              CIP
                                                              AC

Reproduced by Colourscan, Singapore
Printed and bound in Italy by Graphicom

# MAMMALS

# CONTENTS

# WHAT IS A MAMMAL?

Giraffe
(female)

Mammals are amazing animals. Some climb through trees, others race across the ground, burrow, swim, or even fly. They come in many shapes and sizes, too. A giraffe is tall, a mouse is small, and a platypus looks like an otter with a duck's bill. So what makes them all mammals? They are hairy and feed their babies milk. You are a mammal, too.

**Small Start**
A few furry animals scurried between the feet of dinosaurs 195 million years ago.

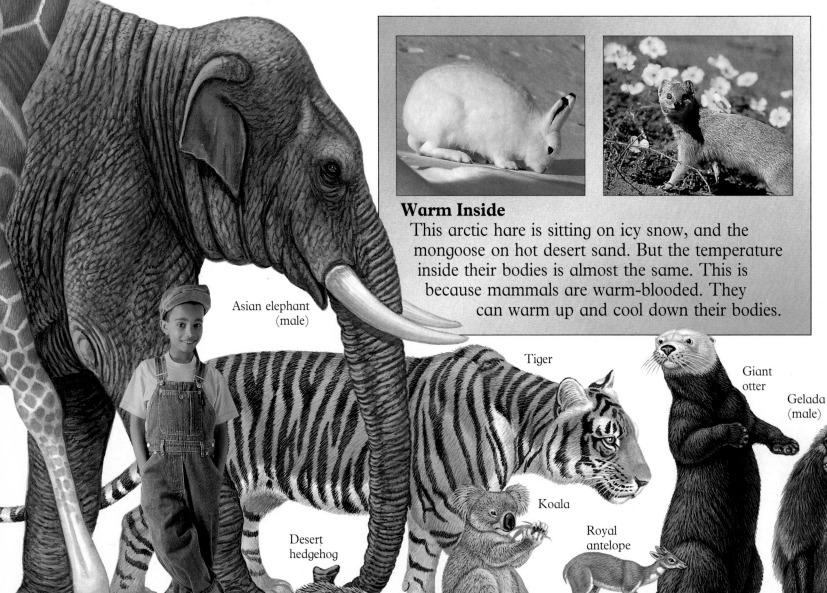

**Warm Inside**
This arctic hare is sitting on icy snow, and the mongoose on hot desert sand. But the temperature inside their bodies is almost the same. This is because mammals are warm-blooded. They can warm up and cool down their bodies.

Asian elephant
(male)

Tiger

Giant
otter

Gelada
(male)

Koala

Desert
hedgehog

Royal
antelope

6

## Odd Mammals Out

Most mammals are born live, not hatched from eggs. Only two types of mammals lay eggs: platypuses and hedgehoglike echidnas. Platypus eggs hatch after just ten days. The babies are then fed on milk for four months.

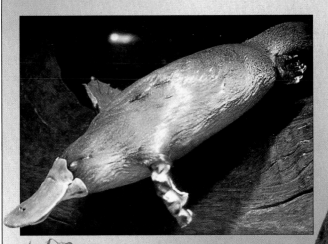

*Platypus eggs are soft and the size of marbles.*

*Ocelots are in danger of disappearing forever because they are killed for their fur coats. More than 550 mammal species are threatened with extinction.*

Giant panda

Little brown bat

Black-tailed jackrabbit

Golden mice

*This is an ocelot. There are more than 4,000 other species of mammals.*

*Mammals are the only animals to have ear flaps.*

*All mammals breathe air into lungs.*

*The lower jaw is made up of one piece of bone.*

*All mammals have hair – even whales. They have hairy lips!*

*Female ocelots give birth, after a 70-day pregnancy, to up to four kittens.*

*Inside the body there is a frame of bones, called a skeleton.*

*Fat keeps in the body's heat.*

## Baby Food

Female mammals make milk in their mammary glands. With nothing to do but sleep, play, and suck milk, their babies grow quickly.

7

# MARSUPIALS

A marsupial is an animal that has a pocket, called a pouch, for carrying its babies. Inside this nursery, the baby is safe and has milk to drink. Today, almost all mammals with pouches live in Australia, but 100 million years ago, they lived all over the world. Most marsupials died out when the more modern mammals developed, such as horses, cats, and rats. Marsupials survived in Australia because the "new" mammals could not reach this isolated island. Kangaroos are the most famous marsupials, but there are also marsupial "mice" and "dogs."

Australia

*Like deer, kangaroos have long faces to make room for their big, flat, grass-grinding teeth.*

**Female red kangaroos** are three feet (one meter) tall. Males are twice as big. They live in Australia.

*Kangaroos can't walk backward!*

*Female red kangaroos are called blue fliers because they have blue-gray fur and bounce faster than the red males.*

*The tail helps it balance as it bounds along.*

*A kangaroo licks a bald spot on its arms to cool down! As the saliva dries, it takes heat away.*

*Only females have pouches – males don't need them because they don't have babies!*

*The baby, or joey, hops into the pouch if it sees an eagle or dingo.*

**Hop to It!**
A kangaroo's back legs are so big that it would fall on its face if it ran. So it hops. A red kangaroo can bounce along at 40 miles (65 km) per hour.

*Huge leg muscles*

## Missing Marsupial

The last Tasmanian wolf is thought to have died in a zoo in 1936. It was striped like a tiger and had a thick tail like a kangaroo's. Farmers shot them all because they ate sheep.

## Bitty Baby

A newborn wallaby looks like a red bean! It is less than .8 inches (2 cm) long and has no legs, hair, or eyes. Like all marsupials, it continues to grow in a pouch, not inside the mother's body.

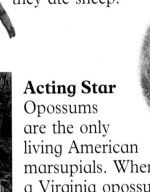

*Birth*

*The "bean" squirms through the forest of hair by waving its stumpy arms.*

*Three minutes later, it reaches the pouch.*

*It hooks onto a nipple and starts to suck milk.*

## Acting Star

Opossums are the only living American marsupials. When a Virginia opossum is attacked, it sticks out its tongue, lies very still, and pretends to be dead – it plays possum!

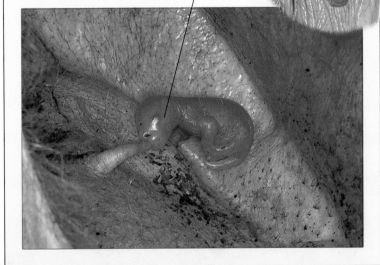

## Hold On Tight

This baby koala is too big to fit inside its mother's pouch, so it clings to her fur as she clambers through the eucalyptus leaves!

## Mammals with Pouches

Tasmanian devil

Honey possum

Numbat

Ring-tailed rock wallaby

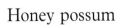

# TOOTHLESS MAMMALS

Anteaters and pangolins have no teeth. Armadillos and aardvarks have small "pegs" at the back of the mouth, but no big, biting teeth – they couldn't bite into a crunchy apple as you can. Tough teeth just aren't needed for licking up ants and termites. Sloths have a few teeth, but they don't have tough enamel on them. Thirty-seven species of these weird, wonderful mammals survive, mainly in South America.

*Ant*

## Ant Scratchings
A pangolin can't get its claws between its scales to scratch. So this "walking pine cone" lets ants climb over its body and eat the insects that cause the itch. When it wants to wash off the ants, it wades into a river. Then it eats the drowned ants!

*Tough plates of horn protect the soft body.*

*Armadillos sniff out ants and termites.*

**Naked-tailed armadillos** are 6 inches (15 centimeters) tall. They live in Guatemala, Belize, and Venezuela.

*This armadillo escapes from danger by quickly digging a tunnel with its huge claws. Some armadillos roll into a ball instead!*

## Sticky Lick
An anteater's tongue is as long as your arm and covered in sticky saliva.

*Anteaters eat more than 30,000 ants a day!*

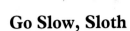

### Creepy-crawly Coat

A sloth is slow, but its coat is full of life! Moths live on its hairy coat. Caterpillars that hatch from the moths' eggs eat tiny plants that grow in grooves in the sloth's hairs.

### Go Slow, Sloth

Three-toed sloths are the slowest of all mammals. When they drag themselves along the ground, they travel just over six feet (two meters) a minute – half the speed of a tortoise!

### Mammals That Can't Bite

### Animal Jigsaw

An aardvark has a body like a pig's, a tail like a kangaroo's, ears like a rabbit's, and it licks up ants and termites like an anteater. But it is not related to any of these other mammals.

Nine-banded armadillo

Giant anteater

*It gulps air into its stomach to help it float across a river!*

*The plates are linked by leathery skin. The armadillo could not bend its body without these joints in its suit of armor.*

*This is the only species of armadillo that doesn't have an armored tail.*

Giant pangolin

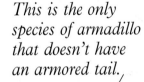

*This part is not armor-plated. It is covered in soft hairs.*

*When this naked-tailed armadillo is older, it will lose its pink color and turn almost black.*

Two-toed sloth

# INSECTIVORES

Insectivores are sharp-toothed, long-nosed animals that munch insects, worms, slugs, and snails! Their busy little bodies lose heat easily, so they need to eat a lot. The food they eat produces the energy needed to keep them warm. But how do insectivores survive winters, when there are fewer insects to eat? Shrews search through rotting leaves, and most manage to find enough food. Moles stay underground, and hedgehogs spend cold winters in a deep sleep, called hibernation.

**A Bite for Lunch**
The water shrew is one of the few poisonous mammals. Its saliva can kill frogs, but not people!

**How Hungry?**
Imagine having to eat a pile of food that weighs twice as much as you do – shrews have to do this every day!

*The tiny eyes are covered by fur. A mole sees poorly – it can just about tell the difference between light and dark.*

*Little bumps on its tail and its nose help this European mole sense where it is going.*

*A mole's wide front feet are shaped like spades – ideal for digging.*

*Molehill*

*The grass nest is the size of a football.*

*Worms burrow into the tunnel and are caught by the mole.*

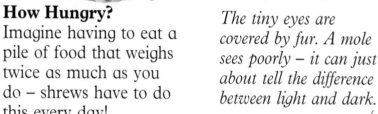

*Moles turn around by doing forward rolls. If the tunnel is too narrow, they run backward.*

*Moles live alone. This worm thief will soon be chased away.*

*A mole eats more than 50 worms a day! Live ones are stored in a larder.*

## Greedy Guts

Shrews often eat animals that are bigger than themselves. This juicy worm will fill this one's tummy for two or three hours!

## Worms in a Week

Streaked tenrecs grow up faster than any other mammals. They stop drinking milk and start to eat worms when they are only six days old.

**Insect-Eaters**

Golden mole

*A hedgehog can stay rolled up for hours.*

*Head*

## Roll Up, Roll Up!

Fearless hedgehogs don't run away from danger – they stick out their spines and roll into a ball. No one wants to eat a mouthful of needles!

Desman

*Some foxes and badgers have learned to push hedgehogs into puddles to make them unroll!*

Star-nosed mole

*The hedgehog's skin is larger than its body. When it curls up, it can pull its prickly skin over its head!*

Solenodon

*Spines are just stiff, hollow hairs.*

*One-week-old baby shrews hold on to one another so that they don't get lost.*

White-tailed shrews

*Adult European hedgehogs have more than 5,000 needle-sharp spines.*

# WEASELS AND MONGOOSES

Many mammals eat meat. Those that have special teeth for killing and eating other animals are known as carnivores. Long front teeth, called canines, are used like daggers to stab, and scissorlike back teeth slice meat off bones. Although tigers and wolves are huge, most carnivores are in fact small. Weasels, skunks, and their relatives, the mongooses, are fierce – they rip their prey apart in a flurry of fur and teeth.

*Badger's canine*

### Tiny but Tough
The American least weasel is the smallest carnivore in the world. It weighs about as much as ten sugar cubes.

*A badger's sense of smell is more than 700 times better than yours!*

*Black and white stripes look like shadows in the dark and make badgers hard to see.*

*Like all members of the weasel family, badgers have long, tube-shaped bodies – ideal for moving through tunnels.*

*Ear*

*Slugs and rats will do, but worms are a badger's favorite food – it eats hundreds each night!*

*Badgers' wiry hair used to be made into bristles for brushes.*

### Fur Coats for Mink
Many mammals are killed for their furry coats. Today there are not enough mink left in the wild to trap, so they are raised on fur farms.

*The powerful jaws can crunch big bones.*

*Short legs*

**Eurasian badgers** are 12 inches (30 centimeters) tall. They live in Europe and Asia.

*Badgers sharpen their big digging claws on trees.*

*The mongoose bites the cobra's head to kill it.*

*One bite from a cobra's fangs can kill a mongoose.*

### Teeth Beat Fangs
A brave, swift mongoose can defeat a cobra! While the snake lifts up its head to spit its poison, the mongoose darts in and clamps its canine teeth around the snake's neck.

*Even when it is knocked off its feet, the mongoose does not let go.*

### Big Squirt
All small carnivores smell, but a stripy skunk stinks! When it is threatened, it lifts up its tail and squirts out two jets of horribly smelly liquid.

### Meerkats on the Menu!
Many small carnivores are eaten by bigger meat-eaters. Meerkats, a type of mongoose, eat scorpions and snakes, but they have to watch out for foxes or they themselves will be eaten.

*This tiny mouse-killer can squeeze through a ring!*

### Better Safe than Sorry
Giant otters in the muddy Amazon river eat most fish headfirst, but they leave the biting jaws of the piranha until last!

### Small Carnivores

Zorilla

American least weasel

Banded palm civet

African linsang

# CATS

Cats are carnivores. Most creep up on their prey by sneaking slowly and silently through the undergrowth. Then, suddenly, they will hurl themselves onto their surprised victim. The sharp canine teeth quickly deal the deadly blow. The biggest cat of all, the tiger, can eat 55 pounds (25 kg) of meat in a meal! But this terrifying animal never meets the lion, the king of the cats, because lions live in Africa and tigers in Asia.

*A cheetah can accelerate as quickly as a Ferrari car*

Tigers

**Bright Eyes**
When light shines on a cat's eyes, they glow like the reflectors on the back of a bike. This happens because the light bounces back off a special layer in the cat's eyes. This layer collects light. It helps cats see six times better than you in dim light.

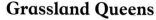

**Aerial Ambush**
All cats climb trees. This spotty jaguar is waiting to drop down on a passing peccary or tapir. It will even tackle giant alligators.

**Grassland Queens**
Lions are the cat oddballs because they live in groups called prides. The male lion is often called the "king of the jungle," but lions do not actually live in jungles – and the females, or lionesses, are in charge.

_Flexible backbone_

_A cheetah can only sprint for 20 seconds because it soon tires._

## Speedy Cat

Cheetahs are the only cats that run down their meals. They can sprint at 60 miles (100 km) per hour and are the fastest mammals.

## Play Fight

Baby cats, or kittens, are playful. They chase one another, leap into the air, and chew twitching tails! This is the way they learn to hunt.

_Sensitive whiskers_

## Really Wild Cat

There are more than 300 million pet cats in the world. They are believed to have been bred from wildcats over 3,000 years ago. This Scottish wildcat is much fiercer than a tame tabby!

**Leopards** are 2 feet (60 cm) tall. They live in Africa and southern Asia.

_The rough tongue can rub meat off bones!_

_Leopards sleep 16 hours a day, usually in short "catnaps."_

_Big cats roar. They can't purr._

_Black leopards, or panthers, can be born to "yellow" parents._

_Panthers are spotty, but their spots are hard to see!_

_Leopards live and hunt on their own. Groups of lions often gang up on them and steal their food._

_A cat combs and cleans its fur coat with its tongue._

_Soft pads let cats creep quietly._

## Put Your Claws In!

Little muscles pull most cats' daggerlike claws into special pockets, to keep them from becoming blunt.

# DOGS

Like all carnivores, dogs eat meat. On its own, a dog can only trap animals that are smaller than itself, but 20 African hunting dogs, working together, can easily catch and kill a zebra. Most dogs have learned this lesson and prefer to hunt in family groups, called packs. The 35 types of wild dogs have often been treated as enemies, not loved like pet dogs. Wolves have been wiped out in many places. Foxes survive only because they are smaller and more cunning.

*All pet dogs have been bred from gray, or timber, wolves. The first dogs were tamed more than 12,000 years ago!*

## Hooooowl!

In the dead of night, the wolves in a pack get together, throw back their heads, and howl. This warns other wolves to keep out of their territory.

**Gray wolves** are about three feet (one meter) tall. They live in the United States, Canada, and northern Asia.

*A wolf can hear a watch ticking over 30 feet (10 m) away.*

*Dogs cool down by panting.*

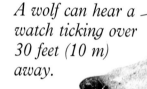

*Pointed canine teeth stab the prey. Cheek teeth slice the meat into pieces that are small enough to swallow.*

*Gray wolves trot more than 35 miles (60 kilometers) a day when they are hunting a moose or an ox.*

## Pack Property

Female African hunting dogs can have as many as 16 babies. These puppies belong to the whole pack, not just the mother. They are even suckled by other females.

*This pup is eight weeks old. It already eats meat, but will not go hunting with the pack until it is six months old.*

## New Neighbor

Red foxes used to live in woods, but many have moved into cities. They scamper through the streets at night searching for fruit and mice – and garbage cans to raid!

## Cleaning Up

Big African dogs, called jackals, love leftover lion food – lions hardly ever finish their dinners! Carnivores that do not kill their own food are called scavengers.

*A fox's tail is called a brush.*

*A gray wolf's thick coat can be any color from white to black!*

*Bushy tail*

## Dog "Talk"

Every dog has to know its place in the pack – they can't all be the leader! Dogs can't talk, so they use body language instead to let one another know whether they make or take orders.

*Dogs wag their tails when they are happy.*

## Win by a Nose

When you smell a flower, you can often tell what sort of flower it is without opening your eyes. Dogs can do much better than this – they can smell who touched the flower the day before!

*Dogs are marathon runners, not sprinters. A wolf can run at only 28 miles (45 kilometers) per hour – much slower than a lion.*

*The pack leader holds his tail upright and snarls.*

*Ankle*

*This dhole does not want to argue, so it rolls on its back.*

*Dogs walk on their toes.*

*The claws stay out all the time.*

# BEARS

Bears are big and usually have thick, shaggy coats. Brown bears are the most common, but giant pandas are more famous. People have argued for years about whether giant pandas are bears or not. Scientists now list the giant panda as a bear – and a very rare one, too! Bears look cuddly, but they are fierce. People have shot so many of these big beasts that today bears survive only in remote areas.

**The Big Sleep**
Bears that live in cold places spend the winter inside warm caves. The females give birth to their tiny cubs while they are fast asleep.

*Polar bear paw print*

**Honey and Grass for Tea?**
Most bears eat all sorts of things – they are omnivores. These are a few of their favorite foods.

Honey

Berries

Grass

**Masters of Disguise**
Polar bears live in the icy Arctic and are the only totally carnivorous bears. Sealskin is their favorite food.

**Open Wide!**
A grizzly bear has a simple way of fishing: it stands in a river and snaps up fish as they leap out of the water.

*The polar bear hides its black nose with its white paw.*

*It sneaks up on the seal by pretending to be an iceberg!*

*The cunning bear springs out of the icy water to kill the surprised seal with one swipe of its huge paw.*

*Half-webbed toes*

*Ringed seal pup*

## Paw Prints

Unlike cats and dogs, bears have flat feet. Their heels touch the ground when they walk.

*A special pad on the panda's paw is used as a sort of thumb. It is used to grasp bamboo shoots.*

*All bears have small, round ears.*

*This big brown bear is over twice the size of a tiger!*

*A bear's face always looks the same – you can't tell whether it is angry or happy!*

### Save the Giant Panda!

There are fewer than 1,000 giant pandas left. It is not going to be easy to save them – females are only fertile for three days a year. They also need to eat 45 pounds (20 kilograms) of one special type of bamboo a day.

*Many bears have rotten teeth. This is because they love sweet foods – especially honey!*

*With their big, strong arms, bears can hug a person to death!*

*Grizzly bears are a type of brown bear. They are called grizzly bears because the tips of their brown hairs are gray, or grizzled.*

**Grizzly bears** stand up to ten feet (three meters) tall. They live in Canada and the United States.

*The front paws can be used as clubs to hit other large animals.*

# APES

There are four kinds of apes: chimpanzees, orangutans, gibbons, and gorillas. They all live for many years, have big brains, lack tails, and can walk upright. Apes are the closest relatives of people.

Playful

Begging for food

Orangutan (male)

Gorillas are the biggest and strongest apes, but they are gentle giants. Chattering chimps are clever and cute but much more dangerous – they even kill deer and monkeys to eat! Family life is important to all these intelligent animals. Chimps cuddle and even shake hands when they meet.

**Playtime**
Baby chimps take a long time to grow up. Their mothers feed them milk for five or six years – so they have plenty of time to play.

**Brainy Beast**
Chimps are one of the few animals to use tools. They use leaves as sponges! They soften handfuls of leaves by chewing them, then use them to soak up water.

**Go Bananas**
Gorillas really do eat bananas. They also like nettles, giant celery, and banana leaves.

*Apes walk on their knuckles.*

**Walk like an Ape**
All apes can stand on just two feet, but they usually walk on all fours, like this.

**Not a Word**
The chimp is one of the few mammals that can make faces to show its feelings.

Frightened

Angry

**Holding Hands**
You can pick things up because you are able to fold your thumb across your hand. Apes and monkeys have these useful, "opposable" thumbs, too.

*Like you, apes have sensitive hands.*

**Male gorillas** are about 5.5 feet (1.7 meters) tall, when standing upright, but females are only half this size. Gorillas live in Africa.

*An orangutan's big toes can grip things, too!*

*Gorillas have about the same number of hairs as you. They look more hairy because their hair is long and grows all over their bodies.*

*Big brain*

*Gorillas can climb trees, but they spend most of the day lazing on the ground.*

**Is It a Bird?**
Every night, orangs build a cozy nest to sleep in. It takes just five minutes to build a mattress of branches and a blanket of leaves.

*Apes see things in color – just like you.*

*Baby gorillas learn to crawl at ten weeks, climb at five months, and walk at eight months. They may live to be 40.*

*All apes can sit and stand up straight.*

# MONKEYS

Monkeys are primates. It is easy to tell them apart from the advanced primates, people and apes, because they have tails. Some, such as mandrills, live on the ground, but most monkeys are light enough to jump or swing through the trees. They always look before they leap, though, because there is danger all around. Large eagles may swoop down, and leopards lurk below. If they lose their footing, monkeys may plunge up to 200 feet (60 meters) to the ground. That's like falling from the 13th floor of a building!

Squirrel monkey

**Built to Balance**
If you start to lose your balance, you can use your arms to steady yourself. Monkeys use their tail instead – leaving their arms free for climbing

**Keep It Clean!**
These rhesus monkeys are lining up to have insects and dirt picked out of their fur. They even pick one another's teeth clean! This grooming helps to keep them tidy and also to be good friends.

*Groups of monkeys are called troops.*

**Face to Face**

**Telltale Tail**
Ring-tailed lemurs are primitive primates and live in troops as monkeys do. They keep together in tall grass by pointing their tails upward.

*This lemur is looking for a tail to follow!*

Mandrill (male)          Proboscis monkey (male)

Bald uakari              Cotton-top tamarin

## A Gripping Tail

Many South American monkeys have three "arms" – their tails are prehensile, so they can hold on to things. A spider monkey can hang by its strong tail, leaving both hands free for feeding.

*All primates, including you, see in color.*

*Narrow chest*

*Both eyes face forward to spot safe landing places!*

*Mane of soft, silky hair*

*Monkeys are not fussy eaters. They eat fruit, flowers, lizards, butterflies, and even frogs' legs!*

*Monkeys' legs are shorter than their arms.*

*This tamarin weighs only 20 ounces (600 grams), so it is light enough to scamper across small branches without breaking them.*

*People have chopped down so many of the trees golden lion tamarins live in that there are fewer than 200 of these monkeys left. They are in danger of extinction.*

*Hairy tail*

**Golden lion tamarins** are 9 inches (22 cm) tall. They live in Brazil.

## Bathtime

Japanese snow monkeys never get cold feet. They spend much of the winter sitting in pools of hot water that bubble up from beneath the icy ground.

# BATS

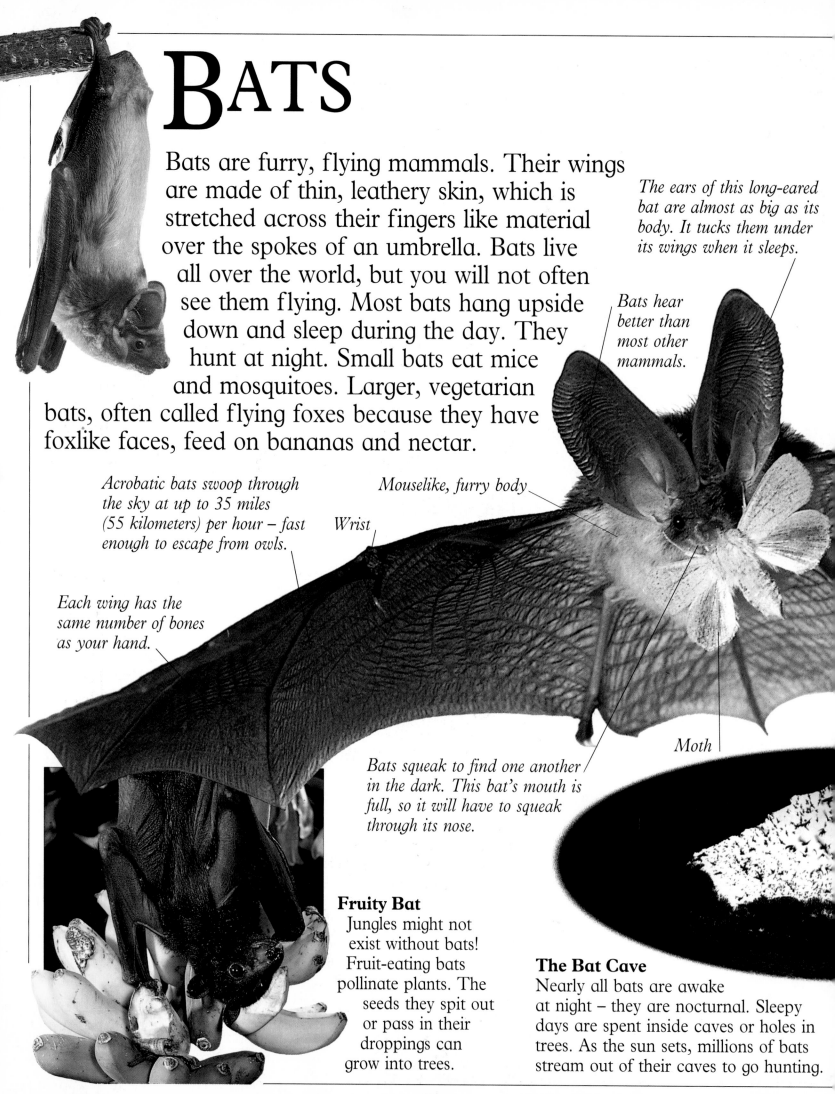

Bats are furry, flying mammals. Their wings are made of thin, leathery skin, which is stretched across their fingers like material over the spokes of an umbrella. Bats live all over the world, but you will not often see them flying. Most bats hang upside down and sleep during the day. They hunt at night. Small bats eat mice and mosquitoes. Larger, vegetarian bats, often called flying foxes because they have foxlike faces, feed on bananas and nectar.

*The ears of this long-eared bat are almost as big as its body. It tucks them under its wings when it sleeps.*

*Bats hear better than most other mammals.*

*Acrobatic bats swoop through the sky at up to 35 miles (55 kilometers) per hour – fast enough to escape from owls.*

*Mouselike, furry body*

*Wrist*

*Each wing has the same number of bones as your hand.*

*Bats squeak to find one another in the dark. This bat's mouth is full, so it will have to squeak through its nose.*

*Moth*

### Fruity Bat
Jungles might not exist without bats! Fruit-eating bats pollinate plants. The seeds they spit out or pass in their droppings can grow into trees.

### The Bat Cave
Nearly all bats are awake at night – they are nocturnal. Sleepy days are spent inside caves or holes in trees. As the sun sets, millions of bats stream out of their caves to go hunting.

## Camping Bats

Imagine having to build a new house every night – tent bats do! These small, white bats nibble through the middle rib of a palm leaf until it droops down to form a tiny tent. The bats hang underneath, out of the wind and rain.

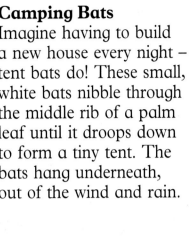

### The Smallest Mammal

The hog-nosed bat can fit in the palm of your hand. Its body is 1.2 inches (3 cm) long, and it has a wingspan of just 6 inches (15 cm). It weighs less than one grape.

*This is a thumb. Bats use their thumbs as combs to groom their fur and as hooks to hold on to things.*

*The wing can be used as a scoop to catch flying insects.*

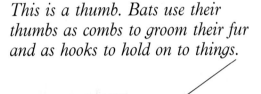

*Long finger*

**Long-eared bats** have a wingspan of 11 inches (28 cm). They live in northern Europe.

### Fangs for Dinner!

Vampire bats love the taste of blood. This one has sliced open the foot of a sleeping chicken with its sharp teeth. It will lap up about one tablespoonful of blood.

### Sounds Tasty

Many bats don't use their eyes to see – they use their voices and ears instead! American fishing bats make clicking noises as they fly over ponds. When these sounds bounce back off ripples, they know that a fish is near the surface.

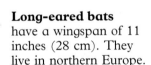

*The bat hears the tiny echo and swiftly swoops down to grab the fish.*

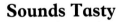

# SMALL RODENTS

A rodent is an animal that gnaws with sharp, chisel-shaped teeth. Most are mouselike and vegetarian: they nibble plant stems, seeds, and roots. Forty percent of all mammals are rodents. They live all over the world – from African jungles, where crested rats climb trees, to scorching deserts, where jerboas hop across the sand. House mice have even hitched rides on boats and lived in huts in Antarctica.

Dormouse

*These newborn, rubbery, wriggling mice can only squeak, sleep, and suckle.*

## Moving House

Every three or four years, thousands of lemmings dash from their overcrowded homes. Many die in the frantic search for new places to live and feed.

## A Plague of Rats

Every year, millions of nibbling rats wreck one-fifth of the world's crops!

*Many brown rats live in sewers. They use their feet as paddles when they swim and can tread water for three days!*

*The greasy fur leaves dirty marks on things it touches.*

*Flat teeth at the back of a rat's mouth grind up grass and grain.*

*Scaly tail*

*After walking through dirt, rats walk over food. This is how they spread diseases.*

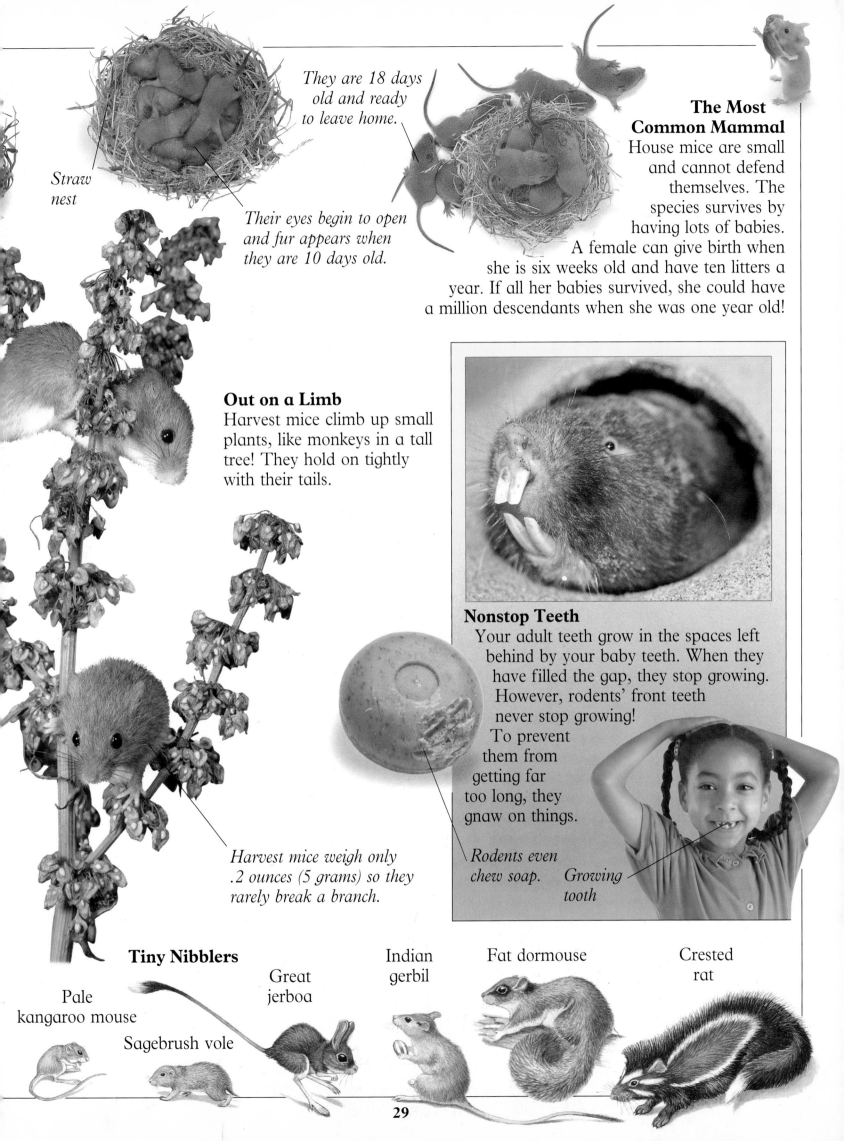

*Straw nest*

*They are 18 days old and ready to leave home.*

*Their eyes begin to open and fur appears when they are 10 days old.*

## The Most Common Mammal

House mice are small and cannot defend themselves. The species survives by having lots of babies. A female can give birth when she is six weeks old and have ten litters a year. If all her babies survived, she could have a million descendants when she was one year old!

## Out on a Limb

Harvest mice climb up small plants, like monkeys in a tall tree! They hold on tightly with their tails.

*Harvest mice weigh only .2 ounces (5 grams) so they rarely break a branch.*

## Nonstop Teeth

Your adult teeth grow in the spaces left behind by your baby teeth. When they have filled the gap, they stop growing. However, rodents' front teeth never stop growing! To prevent them from getting far too long, they gnaw on things.

*Rodents even chew soap.*

*Growing tooth*

## Tiny Nibblers

Pale kangaroo mouse

Sagebrush vole

Great jerboa

Indian gerbil

Fat dormouse

Crested rat

# LARGE RODENTS

Most rodents are small and look like mice, but some are much bigger. There are two sorts of large rodents – those that look like squirrels, and those, such as porcupines, that look like pigs. All rodents keep their teeth from growing too long by gnawing, but beavers and prairie dogs chew so much that they can transform the countryside.

Chipmunks

**Size of a Sheep!**
The capybara is the largest rodent in the world. It is a relative of the guinea pig.

**The Lion Lost**
A porcupine will run backward and stick its quills into an attacker's face!

*A porcupine can hear a juicy fruit drop to the ground several yards away.*

*Hollow, striped quill*

*The nest, or drey, is the size of a football.*

*African porcupines chew old bones to keep their teeth sharp.*

*Angry African porcupines stamp their back feet to rattle their quills. This warns other animals to go away.*

**Giant Nibblers**

*The sharp quills only stick up when the porcupine is attacked.*

European red squirrel

Chinchilla

Rock cavy

Springhaas

Woodchuck

**Planting Trees**
Squirrels bury nuts to eat later. Those that they can't find again may grow into trees.

*A squirrel's strong jaws can crack open acorns.*

*Warm, leafy lining*

**Digging "Dogs"**
Prairie dogs live in underground towns! These towns usually have a population of about 1,000, but one in Texas had more than 400 million prairie dogs in it.

*The "garden" is weeded.*

*"Watchdog"*

*Prairie dogs touch teeth when they meet.*

*When it sleeps, the squirrel wraps its bushy tail around it like a blanket.*

**Squirreled Away**
European red squirrels don't scamper through gardens and parks like their gray American cousins. They are shy and hide from people in forests.

*Gray squirrels race through the trees at up to 18 miles (30 km) per hour.*

*A gray squirrel can leap more than 20 feet (6 meters) from one tree to another.*

*Squirrels can walk up and down the sides of trees to reach their nests.*

*A hole in the roof lets in air.*

*The house, or lodge, is the size of a large tent.*

*The underwater entrance keeps out enemies.*

*Food store*

**Timber!**
American beavers are excellent builders. They bite through trees with their teeth and then pile up the logs in a river. Behind this dam, a pond soon forms, where they can build their home.

*Dam*

# MARINE MAMMALS

Not all mammals live on land – some swim in the sea. Sea cows, narwhals, and all other marine mammals have to come to the surface to take in air because, unlike fish, they do not have gills for breathing. Walruses, sea lions, seals, and otters can climb out of the water. Sixty-five million years ago, the ancestors of whales and dolphins could walk, too. Skeletons of some whales still have leg bones!

*Bowhead whale's "leg"*

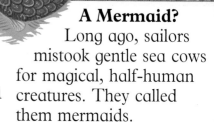

**A Mermaid?**
Long ago, sailors mistook gentle sea cows for magical, half-human creatures. They called them mermaids.

## Blushing Blubber
When a walrus sunbathes, blood rushes to the surface of its skin to cool it down, and it turns pink!

*Sea lions can sit up because they can twist their back flippers forward.*

*This brown walrus has just left the icy water.*

*Five long toes, joined by skin, form a flipper.*

**California sea lions** grow up to 8 feet (2.4 meters) long. They live in the Pacific Ocean.

## Underwater Birth
Baby blue whales are the biggest babies in the world! They are over 1,000 times heavier than human babies.

*Whales are born tail first to keep them from drowning.*

*The baby, or calf, rests on its mother's back and takes its first breath.*

*The playful calf drinks 155 gallons (600 liters) of milk a day. It doubles its weight in the first week.*

*A sea lion's large eyes can see only in black and white.*

*When it dives, the sea lion closes its nostrils and blocks its windpipe with its tongue. This keeps it from swallowing water when it snaps up a squid, fish, or octopus.*

*Ear flap*

*Sea lions bark!*

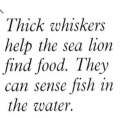

*Thick whiskers help the sea lion find food. They can sense fish in the water.*

*A sea lion's smooth body can speed through the sea at 25 miles (40 kilometers) per hour.*

*Waterproof, oily hair*

## Hope for the Future

Whales are so mysterious and massive that people will pay to see, or even stroke, a wild whale. Perhaps hunters will stop killing whales when they find they can make more money out of tourism.

*The front flippers push the sea lion through the sea.*

## Sea "Bird"

Beluga whales used to be called sea canaries because they chirp like birds. They can pull their lips into all sorts of shapes to squeal, whistle, and "moo," too!

*A thick layer of fat, called blubber, keeps a sea lion warm.*

## Mighty Milk

Seal's milk is full of fat and is richer than the cow's milk you drink. Elephant seal pups put on over 13 pounds (6 kg) every day.

*This pup has a lot of growing to do – its father weighs over two tons!*

*Father*

*Mother*

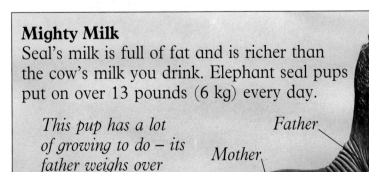

# THE HORSE FAMILY

Almost all the horses in the world are tame. The only wild species left is the Przewalski's horse. It survives in zoos. The commonest wild member of the horse family today is not a horse, but a zebra.

*Przewalski's horse*

Swift, stripy zebras are herbivores. They graze on grass and chew it with their flat back teeth. Horses, zebras, and asses run on the tips of their toes! Each leg ends in a big toe and a hard "shoe," or hoof.

**Desert "Donkeys"**
Wild asses are shy and rare. They live in the dry northern African deserts.

*A zebra's mane stands up straight.*

*The ears twist around to listen for danger.*

**Plains zebras** are up to 4 feet (1.2 m) tall at the shoulder. They live in Africa.

*A zebra can see in color during the day and as well as an owl at night!*

**Best Friends**
Zebras and wildebeests like to live together. The zebras keep watch, while the wildebeests sniff the air for lions.

*Wildebeests eat the short grass left by the zebras.*

*The hoof is just a large toenail!*

*Foals can walk when they are a few minutes old.*

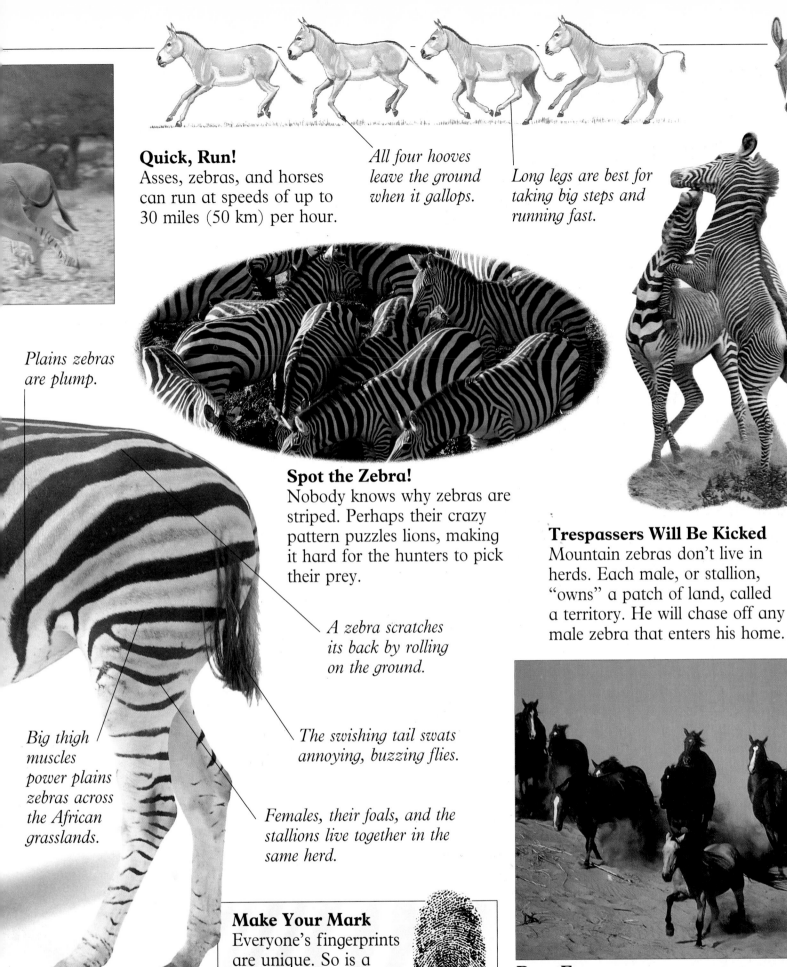

### Quick, Run!
Asses, zebras, and horses can run at speeds of up to 30 miles (50 km) per hour.

*All four hooves leave the ground when it gallops.*

*Long legs are best for taking big steps and running fast.*

*Plains zebras are plump.*

### Spot the Zebra!
Nobody knows why zebras are striped. Perhaps their crazy pattern puzzles lions, making it hard for the hunters to pick their prey.

*A zebra scratches its back by rolling on the ground.*

### Trespassers Will Be Kicked
Mountain zebras don't live in herds. Each male, or stallion, "owns" a patch of land, called a territory. He will chase off any male zebra that enters his home.

*Big thigh muscles power plains zebras across the African grasslands.*

*The swishing tail swats annoying, buzzing flies.*

*Females, their foals, and the stallions live together in the same herd.*

### Make Your Mark
Everyone's fingerprints are unique. So is a zebra's pattern of stripes. Each one wears a different coat! Some even have thin white stripes on a black background.

*There is only one toe inside this hard hoof.*

### Born Free
Some of the world's 75 million tame horses escaped into the wild. The ancestors of these American "wild" horses, or mustangs, belonged to cowboys and Native Americans.

# RHINOS AND TAPIRS

Rhinos and tapirs are related – they both have three toes on each foot, eat only plants, and like to be alone. Apart from size, the main difference between these shy, quiet animals is that the rhino has a horn on the end of its nose. Rhino is short for rhinoceros, which means "horned nose." These ancient animals have lived on Earth for over 55 million years, but may not survive much longer. Rhinos are hunted, and the tapir's forests are being cut down.

**Thick-skinned**
This rare Indian rhino has thick skin, which protects it from spiky forest plants. Deep folds in its knobbly skin make it look as if it is wearing armor.

*Rhinos cannot see things clearly if they are more than 100 feet (30 meters) away.*

*Muscles in this hump hold up the huge head.*

*White rhinos have a second, smaller horn.*

*The horn is made of hair, not bone. It can grow to be as long as a bathtub!*

**Disappearing Rhinos**
In 20 or 30 years' time, rhinos may become extinct. They are being slaughtered so that their hairy horns can be made into dagger handles or crushed into a powder used as a medicine.

*A wide mouth is good for picking big mouthfuls of grass.*

*This four-week-old calf will stay with its mother until the next baby is born in two years' time.*

*Tiny hoof*

## Is It a Rhino?

Rhinos have changed shape and size over a long time. The first ones were the size of big dogs. Twenty million years ago, they were taller than giraffes.

*This rhino was the biggest mammal ever to live on land.*

*Early rhinos looked like tapirs.*

*During the ice age, 15,000 years ago, rhinos were woolly.*

## Charge!

Puffing like a steam train, black rhinos often charge at moving objects they don't like or recognize. Because they are nearsighted, they gallop blindly at anything.

*White rhinos are in fact gray, but they often roll in pale soil, which makes them look white.*

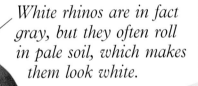

**White rhinos** are 6 feet (1.8 meters) tall. They live in Africa.

*Female rhinos can produce 5 gallons (20 liters) of milk a day.*

*A white rhino can weigh over two tons. It is heavier and bigger than a family car.*

*Rhinos can sleep standing up.*

## Cat Food!

The donkey-sized Malayan tapir is the leopard's favorite food. To escape being eaten, this mother and baby are plunging into the water – they can swim better than cats.

## Hide and Seek

Baby Brazilian tapirs have coats covered in yellowish spots and stripes. This pattern makes them hard to see in the light and shadows of their jungle home.

# HIPPOS, PIGS, AND PECCARIES

Hippo is short for hippopotamus, which means "river horse." Hippos are called river horses because they live in rivers and lakes and eat grass. Pigs and peccaries do not live in rivers, but they enjoy wallowing in mud as much as their huge relatives. Although these water-loving mammals are not carnivores, they are all able to protect themselves. Wild pigs can stab and kill tigers with their tusks, peccaries fight jaguars, and a heavy hippo will tussle with a crocodile or smash into a boat!

**Very Important Pig**
Farmyard pigs have all been bred from wild boars.

**Built-in Suntan Lotion**
Hippo skin oozes tiny blobs of pink liquid. This oil keeps their skin from drying out and also protects them from sunburn.

**Open Wide**
You yawn when you are tired or bored, but male hippos "yawn" when they are angry! Smaller males are frightened off by the big teeth and swim away without starting a fight.

*The eyes and nostrils are high up on a hippo's head. This means it can stick just the top of its head out of the water and still see and breathe.*

*Smooth, almost hairless, skin*

*The tusks, half as long as a yardstick, are sometimes used to stab crocodiles.*

**Hippos** are 5 feet (1.5 meters) tall. They live in Africa.

*This big male hippo weighs as much as 120 eight-year-old children!*

## Lumbering Lawn Mowers

Every night, hippos leave the water and spend five or six hours grazing. They troop back into the water down well-worn paths long before the scorching Sun rises.

## Plucky Peccary

If a mountain lion attacks a group of peccaries, one brave animal runs squealing toward the lion. This peccary dies, but the mothers and babies escape.

## Muddy Buddies

Bush pig

Collared peccary

## Underwater Ballet

Hippos can hold their breath for more than five minutes. This is plenty of time to dive down and tiptoe gracefully across the bottom of a lake.

Hippo

*To keep cool and moist, hippos spend 16 hours a day up to their necks in water.*

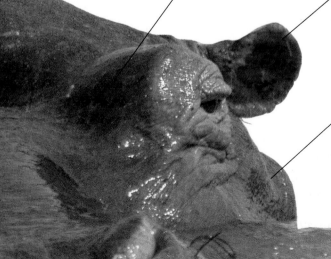

*The hippo shuts its ears and nostrils when it is underwater.*

*There are four toes on each foot.*

*Thick skin protects the hippo from snapping crocodiles.*

Pygmy hippo

*Hippos do eat water lilies, but prefer grass.*

# THE CAMEL FAMILY

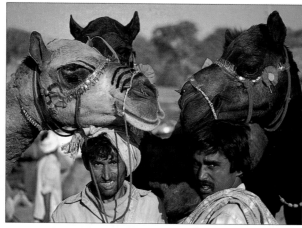

You find camels and their smaller South American relatives, vicuñas and guanacos, on sandy deserts, rocky plains, and bare mountains. They survive in some of the harshest places on Earth. Vicuñas can breathe thin mountain air, and camels can cope with freezing nights and scorching desert days. People have made good use of these animals' amazing survival skills – most are domesticated and work for a living. There are few wild members of the camel family left.

*The fat inside a camel's humps provides food to keep it going during hard times.*

**Domestic Dromedary**
Desert peoples could not survive without their one-humped camels. They are ridden, milked, and eaten. Camel skin is made into shoes, hair is woven into clothes, and dry droppings are used as fuel!

**Swallow That!**
After ten months without a drink, a thirsty camel can gulp down nine big buckets of water in just 15 minutes.

*Partly digested food is brought back up from the rumen to be rechewed.*

*Chewed food travels first into the huge rumen.*

*Third stomach*

*Second stomach*

**Twice as Tasty**
To get all the goodness out of grass, some mammals, such as camels, deer, and cattle, have more than one stomach and chew their food twice!

The ears and nostrils can be pressed flat to keep out sand.

Two rows of eyelashes keep out sand and stop the eyes from freezing on cold desert nights.

A camel doesn't waste water. Liquid from its runny nose drips down the split lip into its mouth!

**Bactrian camels** are 7 feet (2.2 meters) tall. They live in the Gobi desert in Asia.

Camels spit at things that annoy them.

Tough lips can grip thorny desert plants.

Camels hardly ever sweat. This saves water.

### King of the Castle
While the females graze, the male vicuña stands on a rock. If it spots a mountain lion, it whistles, and the fleecy females flee.

Camels roll from side to side when they walk because they lift both legs on one side at the same time.

The two toes spread out to keep the camel from sinking into soft sand.

### Spitting Images

Dromedary

Bactrian camel

Guanaco

Vicuña

### Hard-working Mammals
Llamas and alpacas have been bred by people from wild guanacos. Llamas are milked and used to carry heavy loads. Alpacas are kept for their fine wool.

Alpaca

Llama

# DEER AND GIRAFFES

First year

Third year

Giraffes, reindeer, and all male deer have spikes of solid bone growing out of the tops of their heads. Male deer use their horns to fight for females. The giraffe's bony stumps are covered in skin, but most deer have bigger, bony headgear, called antlers. These are covered in furry skin, or velvet, while they are growing, and they drop off and grow again every year. In just a few months, a moose can grow antlers that are bigger than you!

*Male deer are called bucks or stags.*

*With eyes on the sides of its head, the deer can see all around and easily spot danger.*

*Male and female red deer only meet for a few weeks each year. They usually live in separate herds.*

### No Red Nose
Reindeer live in cold countries. They have thick fur to keep them warm – even their noses are furry! They find food under the snow by digging with their antlers and hooves.

**Red deer** live in Asia and Europe. Males are 4 feet (1.3 m) tall at the shoulder.

### Musk Maker
A male musk deer has a gland on its belly that makes a smelly liquid, called musk. This long-lasting scent is an ingredient of many perfumes.

### Wading In
In the winter, moose eat pine cones. In the summer, they wade into water and munch more than 1,000 salty water plants a day.

Fifth year

Seventh year

**Growing Up**
A red deer stag's antlers drop off every spring and are replaced by a new, bigger, better set. Its heavy headgear takes only about 100 days to grow.

*Bony stump*

*Giraffes are the tallest mammals. Males are about 16 feet (5 meters) high.*

*For six weeks each autumn, males fight with their antlers. The older males, with larger antlers, win the females.*

*Female deer, called does or hinds, do not grow antlers.*

**Legs Apart!**
When a giraffe wants to drink from a pool, it has to stretch its long legs out wide – only then can it reach the ground.

*This winter coat is thick and brown, but a red deer's thin summer coat is more red in color.*

*Red deer eat leaves and grass for 10 to 12 hours a day.*

*Hoof*

**Hide and Spot**
Baby deer, or fawns, have spotted coats for camouflage. They lie still in tall grass and hope that no deer-eating animals see them.

# CATTLE AND ANTELOPES

Cattle, antelopes, and their relatives, goats and sheep, are all bovids. This means that they have horns firmly fixed to the tops of their heads. Horns have a bony core and an outer layer made of the same stuff as your fingernails. Bison graze on grass, but gerenuk antelopes prefer to browse on leaves. Like all bovids, they get goodness out of their poor-quality plant foods by coughing up partly digested food and chewing it a second time. This is called cud chewing.

Gerenuk (male)

*All cattle have four stomachs!*

*These horns are about half as tall as you!*

*This rare antelope, the Arabian oryx, chews the cud as it walks across the desert.*

Arabian oryx

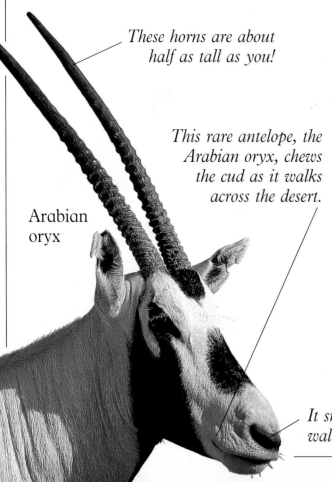

**On the March**
At the onset of the dry season, huge herds of wildebeest walk almost 1,000 miles (1,600 km) to wetter, greener pastures. When the wet season begins, they wander back. These long, yearly journeys are called migrations.

*Like all cattle, bison have split hooves.*

*It sniffs the air for rain and then walks to where the grass is growing.*

44

**Built-in Radiator**
The Tibetan yak lives near the top of the world in the Himalayan mountains. It does not get cold, though, because it has its own central heating system – the moss being digested in its stomach is hot and keeps it warm.

## Heads with Horns

African buffalo (male)

Blackbuck (male)

*This thick winter coat falls off in big clumps during the spring.*

*A dark coat soaks up the Sun's heat. This helps keep the bison warm in cold weather.*

*Male bison fight for females by putting their heads together and pushing. The winner is the one who pushes the other backward.*

*Horns are different from antlers. They never form branches or stop growing, and they are not replaced each year.*

Wild goat (male)

*Male bison weigh more than a small car!*

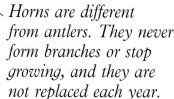

**American bison** are 6 feet (2 m) tall. They live in Canada and the United States.

*Herds of bison spend most of the day eating grass and most of the night chewing!*

Bighorn sheep (male)

# ELEPHANTS

Matriarch

Elephants have huge ears, long noses, and tusks – and weigh more than six cars. They are the biggest land mammals. Herds of elephants shape the land they live in by treading paths wide enough to stop bush fires, by digging wells in dry riverbeds, by fertilizing the ground with dung, and by trampling grass for zebras to eat. They also open up forests by pushing over trees!

## A Family of Females
The leader of a herd of elephants is an old female, called a matriarch. She is followed by all her female relatives and their babies.

*Wrinkles trap water and help keep the elephant cool.*

## It's All Relative
The elephant's closest relative, the hyrax, looks like a guinea pig! Millions of years ago, hyraxes were huge. All that elephants and hyraxes have in common now are tusks, and nails instead of hooves.

## Ivory Towers
Many elephants are shot for their valuable ivory tusks. People have burned huge piles of old tusks to show that they want this cruelty to stop.

*Elephants never stop growing.*

*Tusks are teeth. They grow about 7 inches (17 cm) a year and can be as long as a car!*

## Who's Who?
There are two kinds of elephants.

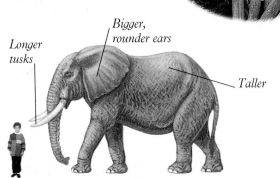

*Humped back*

*Smaller ears*

*Longer tusks*

*Bigger, rounder ears*

*Taller*

*Ankle*

*Elephants eat grass, bark, and leaves for up to 20 hours a day.*

*This toenail is bigger than your whole hand!*

Asian

African

*Males leave their families when they are about 14.*

*Young females act as nannies.*

*An African elephant's ears are almost as big as sheets for a single bed!*

## Stay Cool

Elephants have lots of ways of cooling their big bodies. They can wallow in mud or throw water and dust over their skin. Sometimes they flap their ears like giant fans!

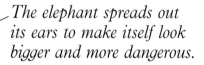

*The elephant spreads out its ears to make itself look bigger and more dangerous.*

*Elephants keep in touch by making deep sounds, called "tummy rumbles."*

*This is one of the first four teeth.*

*Teeth in the sixth, and last, set are bigger than bricks!*

*The trunk is formed from the nose and upper lip. It is used for breathing, smelling, touching, and picking things up.*

*Elephants can live to celebrate their eightieth birthdays!*

## What's Inside?

Elephants may look like they have flat feet, but they really walk on their tiptoes!

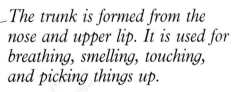

*Toe*

*The heel rests on a fatty cushion.*

## Always Teething!

Apart from tusks, elephants have only four teeth. These molars are replaced every few years. Bigger teeth appear at the back of the mouth and push out the old, worn teeth – like a conveyor belt of teeth!

# GLOSSARY

**Antler** Solid bone that grows out of the top of a mammal's head. Antlers fall off and regrow every year.

**Browsing** Eating the leaves and twigs of trees and small bushes. Giraffes browse.

**Camouflage** Special patterns and colors on an animal's coat that help it hide from danger.

**Canine teeth** Pointed, daggerlike teeth that carnivores, such as tigers, badgers, and wolves, use to grip and kill other animals.

**Carnivore** An animal that mainly eats other animals.

**Digesting** Taking the nutrition out of food to make energy.

**Domesticated** Kept and looked after by people and not living in the wild. Many horses and camels have been domesticated.

**Extinct** Animals that no longer exist or have not been seen for over 50 years.

**Gnawing** The constant chewing carried out by rodents to keep their teeth from growing too long.

**Grazing** Eating grass, usually by biting it down to the ground. Cattle graze.

**Grooming** Cleaning or combing fur. Many animals groom one another.

**Herbivore** An animal that eats plants, but not meat.

**Herd** A group of hoofed animals, such as bison, that feed or move together.

**Hoof** A covering of horn at the end of some animals' feet. Animals that have hooves, such as horses and rhinos, are called ungulates.

**Horn** Bone covered in horn that grows out of antelopes', goats', and cattle's heads. Horns don't fall off.

**Mammary gland** Part of a female mammal's body that produces milk. Babies usually suck this milk through a nipple.

**Marsupial** A mammal that is only partly formed when it is born and then keeps on growing in its mother's pouch.

**Milk** A very rich drink that is full of nutrition. All baby mammals are fed milk by their mothers.

**Molar** Large back tooth used for chewing. A zebra eats grass, so it has a mouthful of molars.

**Molehill** A mound of soil that has been piled up above a mole's underground nest.

**Molting** The regular shedding of one coat of hairs for another. Many mammals, such as camels, have warm winter coats and thinner summer coats.

**Omnivore** An animal that eats both plants and meat. All bears, except polar bears, are omnivores.

**Pack** A group of animals that survive by working together. Dogs hunt in packs.

**Prehensile** Able to grasp on to things. Some mammals have prehensile tails.

**Primate** A group of mammals that includes apes, monkeys, and people. Primates have hands that can grasp and large brains.

**Rumen** A special stomach in many ungulates in which food is partly digested before being brought back up to the mouth to be chewed again.

**Scavenger** An animal that eats meat but that does not usually kill other animals. Scavengers eat other animals' leftovers.

**Species** A type of animal. Gorillas and hippos are different species, so they cannot have babies together.

**Suckling** Nursing, or drinking a mother's milk.

**Territory** The patch of land or water where an animal lives and feeds and which it defends against other animals.

**Trunk** A long, flexible part of an elephant's body made up of the top lip and nose.

**Tusk** A large tooth. Elephants have long tusks.

## Acknowledgments

**Photography:** Andy Crawford, Dave King, Steve Gorton, Tim Ridley, David Rudkin, Harry Taylor, and Jerry Young.

**Illustrations:** Roy Flooks, Ray Hutchins, Stuart Lafford, Ken Lily, Steve Lings, Sean Milne, Richard Orr, Brian Watson, and Phil Weare.

**Model:** Donks Models.

**Thanks to:** Penny Boyd at Burstow Animal Wildlife Sanctuary; Caroline Brooke; The Colour Company; Tina Lewis; Natural History Museum, London; Norrie Carr Model Agency; Scallywags Child Model Agency; Richard Walker; Whipsnade Zoo; Julie Whittaker.

## Picture credits

**Heather Angel:** 43tr; **Ardea:** Jean-Paul Ferrero 34tr, Kenneth W. Fink 35cra, 37cr, Francois Gohier 41cb, Clem Haagner 11cl, J.M. Labat 8c, R.F. Porter 36bl, Adrian Warren 23b, 27cr; **Bruce Coleman Ltd.:** David Austen 40c, Jane Burton 18/19tc, 28cr, Alain Compost 22/23c, Peter Davey 46cl, Adrian Davies 24c, Francisco Erize 30tr, 36br, Jeff Foott 35ca, Steven C. Kaufman 3c, 25bra, Stephen Krasemann 26br, William S. Paton 1c, 17cra, M.R. Phicton 38cr, Dieter & Mary Plage 47cr, Hans Reinhard 38tr, 45tc, Leonard Lee Rue 43br, Norman Tomalin 16cr, John Uisser 29cl, Konrad Wothe 25tl; **Robert Harding Picture Library:** 7br, 42cl; **The Image Bank:** Guido Alberto Rossi 40tc, Jack Ward 35bra; **Frank Lane Picture Library:** Eric & David Hosking 13tl, M. Macri 6c, W. Wisniewski 32clb; **NHPA:** Agence Nature 44c, Henry Ausloos 3tr, 38clb, Stephen Dalton Jacket, 3tlb, 12tr, 12clb, 28c, 28cla, Michael Leech 29l, Lacz Lemoine 34tl, Tsureo Nakamura 33br, Haroldo Palo 37br, S. Robinson 22c, 37tl, Jany Sauvanet 10/11tr, John Shaw 20cr; **Nature Photographers Ltd.:** Paul Sterry 33cra; **Oxford Scientific Films Ltd.:** Animals Animals/Breck P. Kent 44/45c, Hans & Judy Beste 26bl, Michael Fogden 27tl, Renee Lynn 15tr, Joe & Carol McDonald 8/9c, Tom McHugh 7tl, Stan Osolinski 16cra; **Planet Earth Pictures:** K. Ammann 38/39bc, Gary Bell 8/9cb John Bracegirdle 31cr, Jim Brandenburg 18cla, 20tr, Mary Clay 16cl, Richard Coomber 47tc, Ken Lucas 22cl, Richard Matthews 25c, Scott McKinley 42br, Doug Perrine 32/33ca, Ronald S. Rogoff 15c, 19trb, Jonathan Scott 46c, 46/47c, Anup & Manoj Shah 16bc, Peter Stephenson 44bl; **Premaphotos Wildlife:** K.G. Preston-Mafham 6cr; **Survival Anglia Ltd.:** Jeff Foott 39tr, Nick Gordon 15crb, J.M. Pearson bla, Alan Root 9cr, Alan & Jane Root 39cr, Vivek Sinha 42bl; **Zefa:** 22bl, F. Lanting 43c.

l – **left**   c – **center**   b – **bottom**   tl – **top left**   cl – **center left**   bl – **bottom left**   tr – **top right**
cr – **center right**   br – **bottom right**   tc – **top center**   bc – **bottom center**   cb – **center bottom**
ca – **center above**   tlb – **top left below**   trb – **top right below**   cla – **center left above**
clb – **center left below**   cra – **center right above**   crb – **center right below**   bra – **bottom right above**

# INDEX